SCIENCE OF SPORTS

THE SCIENCE OF BASEBALL

WITH MAX AXIOM SUPER SCIENTIST

by David L. Dreier

illustrated by Maurizio Campidelli

Consultant:
Lyle A. Ford
Department Chair
Physics & Astronomy
University of Wisconsin, Eau Claire

CAPSTONE PRESS
a capstone imprint

Graphic Library is published by Capstone Press,
1710 Roe Crest Drive, North Mankato, Minnesota 56003
www.capstonepub.com

Library of Congress Cataloging-in-Publication Data
Drier, David.
  The science of baseball with Max Axiom, super scientist / by David Drier.
      pages cm.—(Graphic Library. The Science of Sports with Max Axiom.)
  Includes bibliographical references and index.
  Summary: "Uses graphic novel format to reveal the scientific aspects at play in the sport of baseball"—Provided by publisher.
  ISBN 978-1-4914-6083-2 (library binding)
  ISBN 978-1-4914-6087-0 (paperback)
  ISBN 978-1-4914-6091-7 (eBook PDF)
  1. Baseball—Juvenile literature. 2. Sports sciences—Juvenile literature. 3. Graphic novels—Juvenile literature. I. Title.
  GV867.5.D76 2016
  796.357—dc23   2015012514

Editor
Mandy Robbins

Designer
Ted Williams

Creative Director
Nathan Gassman

Cover Artist
Caio Cacau

Media Researcher
Jo Miller

Production Specialist
Laura Manthe

Printed in the United States of America in North Mankato, Minnesota.
042015   008823CGF15

TABLE OF CONTENTS

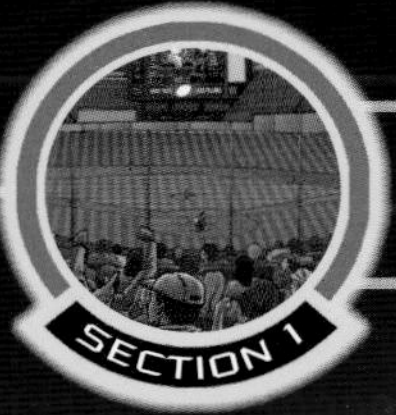
SECTION 1

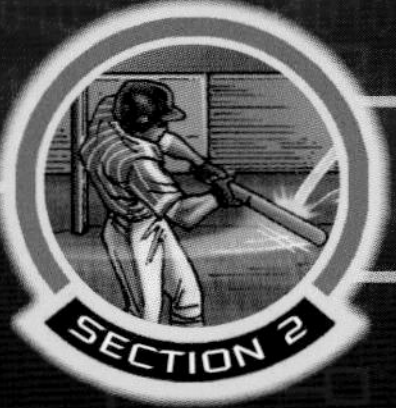
SECTION 2

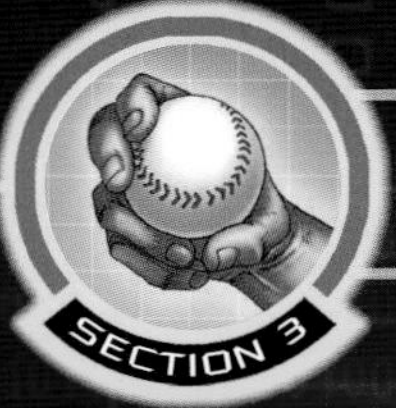
SECTION 3

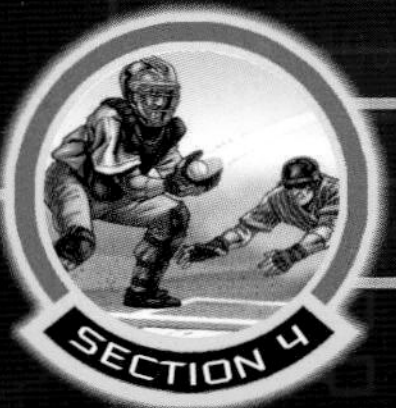
SECTION 4

There's nothing like a baseball game under the lights. A little sports, a little science.

Science?

Sure! Science is everywhere.

Take the lights, for example. They're metal halide lights. They create light by passing an electric arc through a vapor of metal compounds called halides.

Why are they better than regular lights?

They provide brighter, whiter illumination than older lights—perfect for evening baseball.

And notice how crystal clear the sound is coming from the loudspeakers?

NOW BATTING, NUMBER 72—

Let me guess, more science?

You got it! Sound engineers use computers to design stadiums and sound systems in ways that improve the sound quality.

4

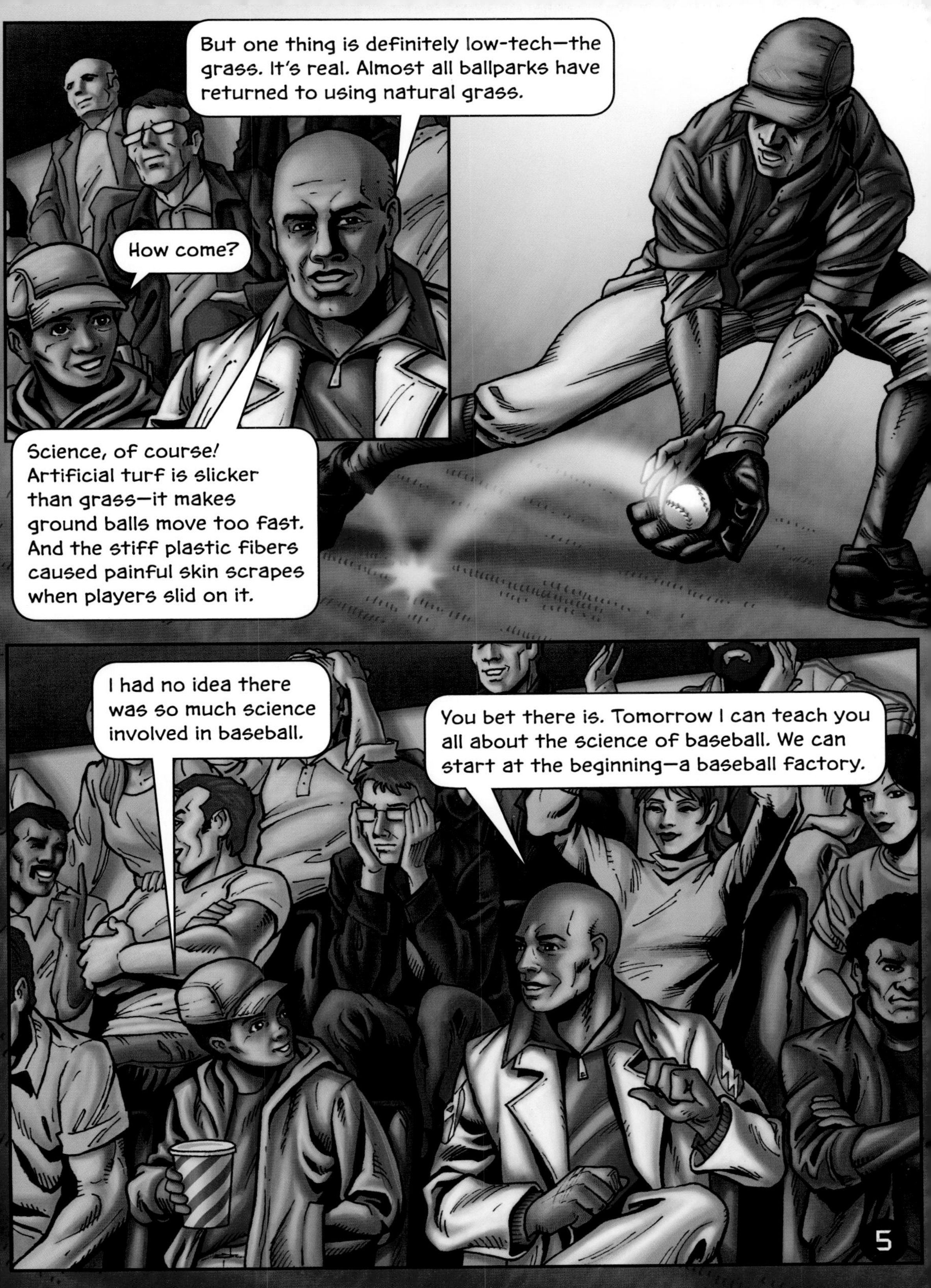
But one thing is definitely low-tech—the grass. It's real. Almost all ballparks have returned to using natural grass.
How come?
Science, of course! Artificial turf is slicker than grass—it makes ground balls move too fast. And the stiff plastic fibers caused painful skin scrapes when players slid on it.
I had no idea there was so much science involved in baseball.
You bet there is. Tomorrow I can teach you all about the science of baseball. We can start at the beginning—a baseball factory.

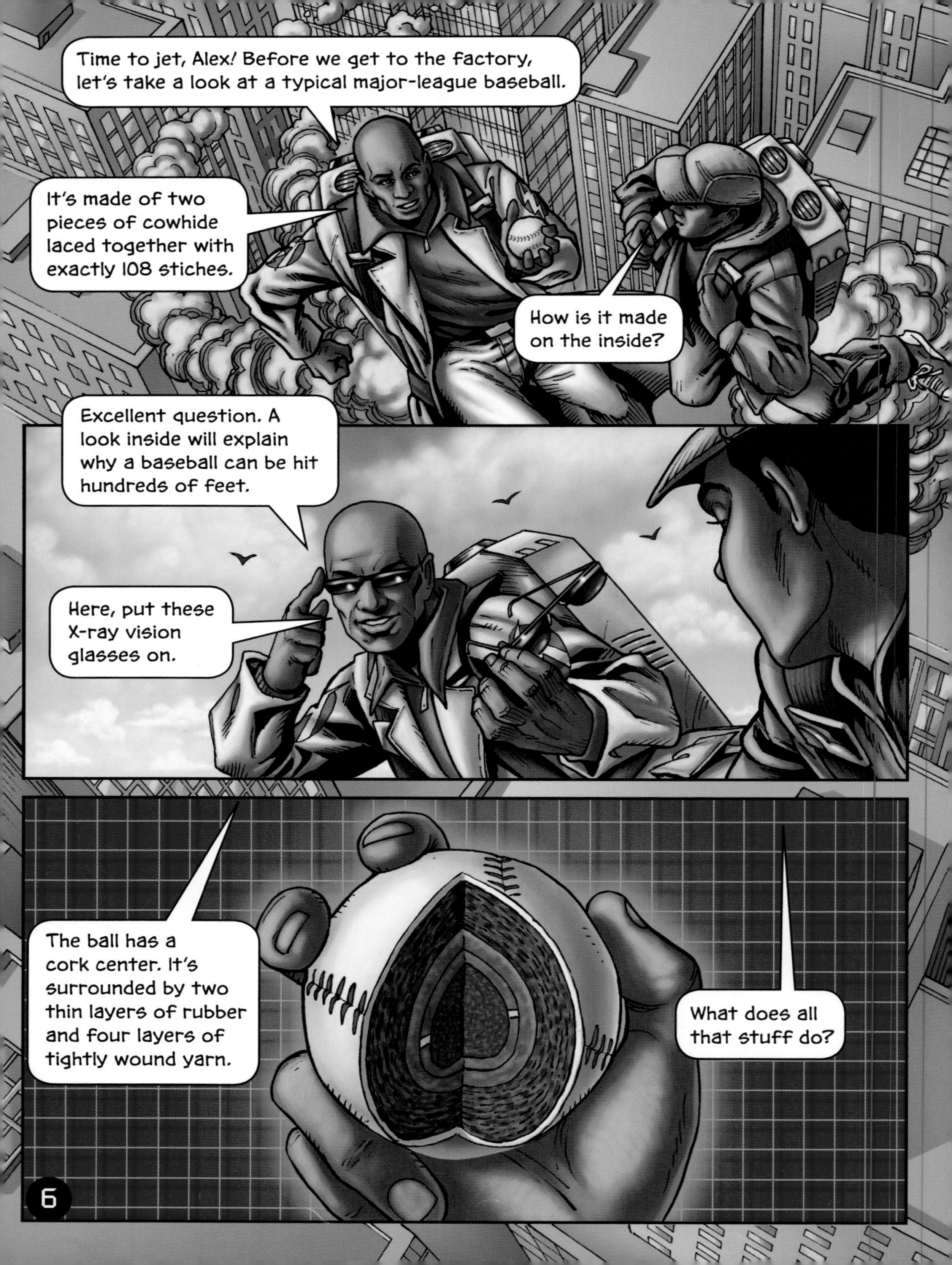

Time to jet, Alex! Before we get to the factory, let's take a look at a typical major-league baseball.
It's made of two pieces of cowhide laced together with exactly 108 stiches.
How is it made on the inside?
Excellent question. A look inside will explain why a baseball can be hit hundreds of feet.
Here, put these X-ray vision glasses on.
The ball has a cork center. It's surrounded by two thin layers of rubber and four layers of tightly wound yarn.
What does all that stuff do?

It produces just the right combination of qualities for a baseball. The ball can be hit hard for a long distance without losing its shape.

Baseball manufacturers test balls chosen at random to make sure they meet standards. The quality-control manager at this plant, Mr. Lively, will show us how it's done.

Hello, Max. And who is this young fellow?

This is my nephew, Alex. He wants to see how you test your baseballs.

Great! The engineers are testing out a batch right now.

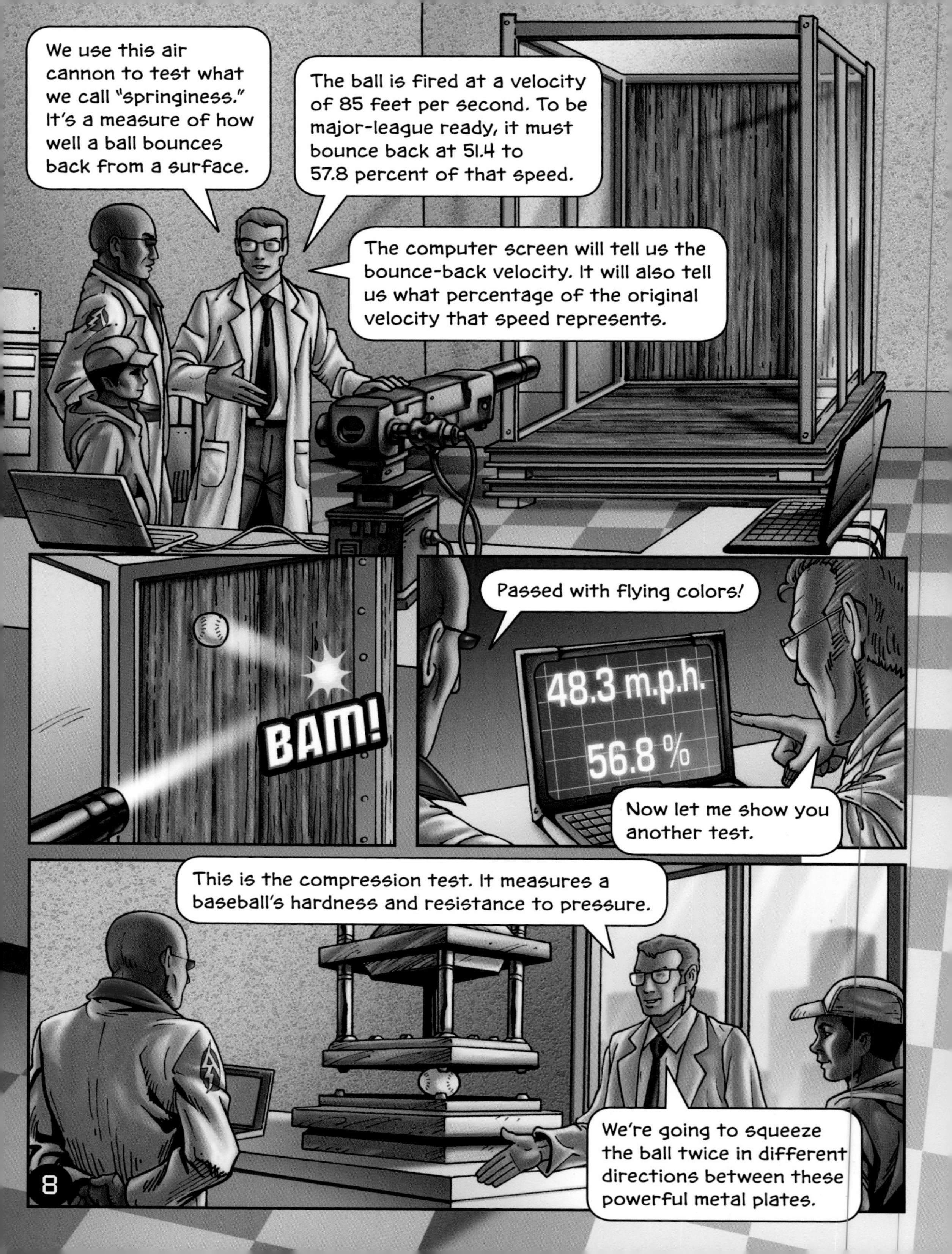
We use this air cannon to test what we call "springiness." It's a measure of how well a ball bounces back from a surface.
The ball is fired at a velocity of 85 feet per second. To be major-league ready, it must bounce back at 51.4 to 57.8 percent of that speed.
The computer screen will tell us the bounce-back velocity. It will also tell us what percentage of the original velocity that speed represents.
BAM!
Passed with flying colors!
48.3 m.p.h.
56.8 %
Now let me show you another test.
This is the compression test. It measures a baseball's hardness and resistance to pressure.
We're going to squeeze the ball twice in different directions between these powerful metal plates.

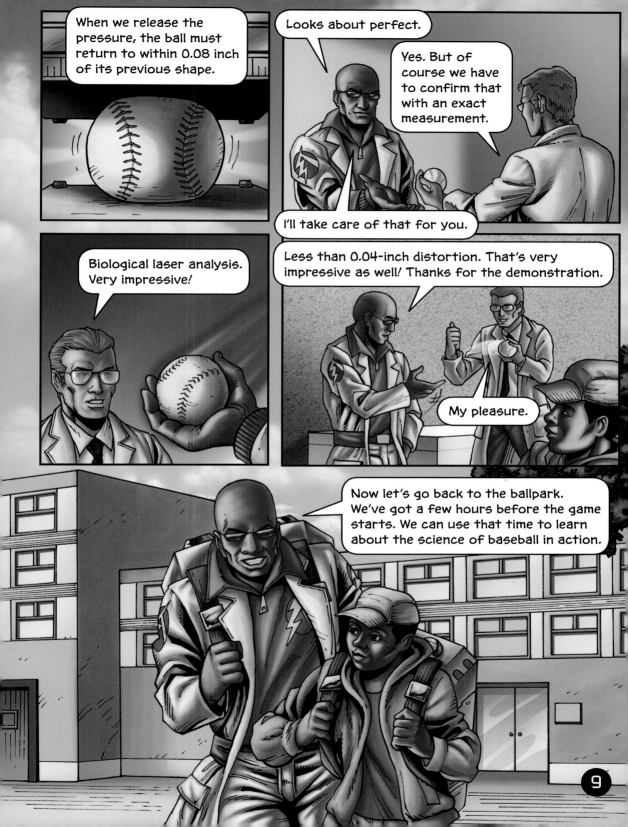

When we release the pressure, the ball must return to within 0.08 inch of its previous shape.

Looks about perfect.

Yes. But of course we have to confirm that with an exact measurement.

I'll take care of that for you.

Biological laser analysis. Very impressive!

Less than 0.04-inch distortion. That's very impressive as well! Thanks for the demonstration.

My pleasure.

Now let's go back to the ballpark. We've got a few hours before the game starts. We can use that time to learn about the science of baseball in action.

Everything centers around the baseball. It gets thrown, hit, and caught. Physics plays a part in every action on the field.

I already know some things about physics. It's part of my science class.

Excellent! Then you should be a fast learner today.

Wow, that's "Whammer" Alvarez. He's great!

So you want to learn about the physics of batting? Let me tell you kid, hitting against a top-notch pitcher is probably the toughest job in sports.

I thought a talk with the team's leading power hitter would be a good start in learning about the physics of hitting.

From where the pitcher releases the ball, there's about 55 feet between the batter and the pitcher.

When a pitcher throws a 95-mile-per-hour fastball, the batter has less than half a second to begin his swing.

How do you make such an instant judgment?

Instinct gained from thousands of times at bat.

Just from the sound, I can tell that one didn't go very far.

A "clunk" means you've hit the ball with the wrong part of the bat. It creates all kinds of vibrations, which means wasted energy.

Studies have shown that a good hitter's brain processes visual information faster than other people do. Whammer sees things in slightly slower motion than you or I do, Alex.

CLUNK!

That's where you want to make contact. It's called the sweet spot. It delivers the most energy possible to the ball.

That's what you want to hear! That one's heading for the stands.

If you want to know more about the physics of batting, you should talk to my friend Miko at Sport City. You can get there and back before game time if you fly.

SMACK!

Whammer said Miko has a passion for baseball and a degree in physics. She can give us the inside scoop on baseball bats.

So, Alex, you're studying physics in school. Have you learned about levers?

Yeah. They multiply a force or change its direction.

Yep! And a baseball bat is a type of lever. You swing the bat around the pivot point. It's located just above your hands. That transfers force from your arms to the ball.

You've had a few swings with that bat, Alex. Now try this one.

The two bats have the same weight, but I think you'll feel a difference between them.

OOPS! This one is harder to swing.

That's because it has a higher swing weight.

Why don't you explain swing weight while we clean up this mess?

So which bat is better?

That's a tricky question. If swung at the same speed, a bat with a higher swing weight will hit the ball with more force. But the other bat will give a batter more control.

Ok. See, with the first bat, the center of mass—the point where the bat would balance—is close to the handle.

The other bat's center of mass is farther from the handle. That makes it harder to swing. That bat has what's called a higher moment of inertia.

So the better bat could be different for every batter.

Exactly. Most batters can't swing all bats at the same speed. They have to find a bat that matches their strength. A lighter bat offers less power but more control. A batter can adjust for more control by sliding his hands up the bat. That's called choking up.

Miko, thanks for the excellent information. But it's time for us to jet!

Where to now, Uncle Max?

We need to get back to the ballpark. The coach is an old pal of mine. I think he can teach us even more about baseball physics.

Batters always risk being hit by a wild pitch. The worst one occurred in 1920. Ray Chapman of the Cleveland Indians died after being hit in the head by a pitch. Even so, it was not until 1971 that batting helmets were required in the major leagues.

Hey Coach! My nephew, Alex, and I have been studying hitting. Seems like the next logical area to cover is running. Could you help us with that?

Of course. I bet you didn't realize that there's more to running than just being fast. The WAY you run is also important.

Really?

You bet. While the infield is clear, let's test different base-running strategies. I'll try running in straight lines first.

8.5 seconds. Amazing! None of my players could run the bases in twice that time!

Well, I am a SUPER scientist. But I think I can do better with a different strategy. Here we go again.

SCREECH!

ZOOM!

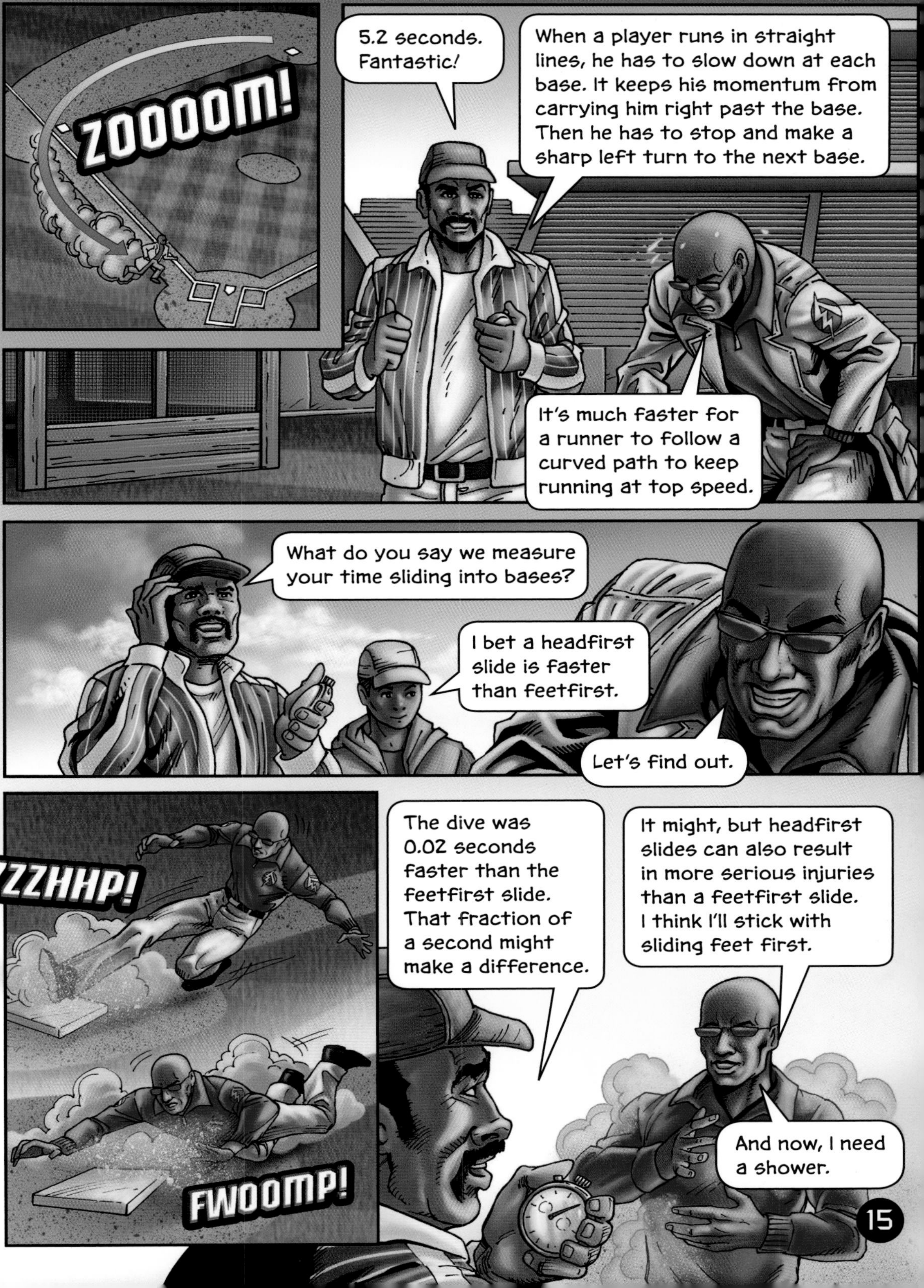
ZOOOOM!
5.2 seconds. Fantastic!
When a player runs in straight lines, he has to slow down at each base. It keeps his momentum from carrying him right past the base. Then he has to stop and make a sharp left turn to the next base.
It's much faster for a runner to follow a curved path to keep running at top speed.
What do you say we measure your time sliding into bases?
I bet a headfirst slide is faster than feetfirst.
Let's find out.
ZZZHHP!
FWOOMP!
The dive was 0.02 seconds faster than the feetfirst slide. That fraction of a second might make a difference.
It might, but headfirst slides can also result in more serious injuries than a feetfirst slide. I think I'll stick with sliding feet first.
And now, I need a shower.

Well, Alex, it's time to shift from offense to defense.

Let's start with pitching. It's all about the pitcher transferring energy from his body to the ball and giving the ball different kinds of spin.

Let's talk with Jake, the pitching coach.

It's only the second inning and already we're running into trouble. That's our top relief pitcher, "Flash" Cameron, warming up.

If you want to learn about pitching, Flash is a great one to watch.

Put on these stop-motion glasses and we'll watch Flash's motions together. Jake, you can give us a running commentary, if you will.

A pitcher goes through a series of motions. They generate a rotational force in his body. Then they transfer that force to the baseball.

And here comes the pitch!

Here Flash is winding up.

Now he's striding forward.

He cocks his arm behind his head.

Then he whips his arm down. This accelerating motion provides a lot of forward momentum as the ball is released.

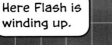

CLICK

CLICK

CLICK

CLICK

A few pitchers have had pitches clocked at a bit more than 100 miles per hour, but that velocity is considered the "speed limit" for sustained pitching. Studies show that throwing a ball much faster than that would cause severe damage to ligaments and tendons.

Finally, Flash decelerates his arm and brings it to a stop across his body.

Why don't you show Alex how some pitches are thrown?

Sure. Each kind of pitch requires a different grip on the ball. Let me show you typical grips for a fastball and a curveball.

Here's the grip for a fastball. It lets you fire the ball straight at the plate at top speed.

This is the grip for a curveball. The grip, along with a snap of the wrist, puts a sideways spin on the ball.

But the grip and the wrist-snap prevent a curve from being thrown as fast as a fastball.

This grip also gives the ball a backward spin. That backspin produces a lifting effect. It keeps the ball from sinking on its way to the plate as much as it normally would.

Have Flash throw a curveball and we'll see what causes the baseball to curve.

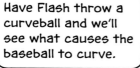

Tap the rim of your glasses twice. That'll switch them to close-up analysis and tracking mode.

Wow!

That's just the beginning. Now watch this. Motion analysis, please.

The spin on a curveball produces what's called the Magnus effect.

It's caused by a high-pressure layer of air produced on the side of the ball that's spinning in the direction that the ball is traveling. There is a low-pressure area on the other side of the ball.

That pressure difference causes a force on the ball from the high-pressure side to the low-pressure side. And that force causes the ball to curve away from a straight line.

Very informative, Max. I guess we've all learned a few things about pitching today.

We've learned that pitchers are masters of physics!

Thanks, Jake! Come on, Alex, let's watch the rest of the game from the stands.

19

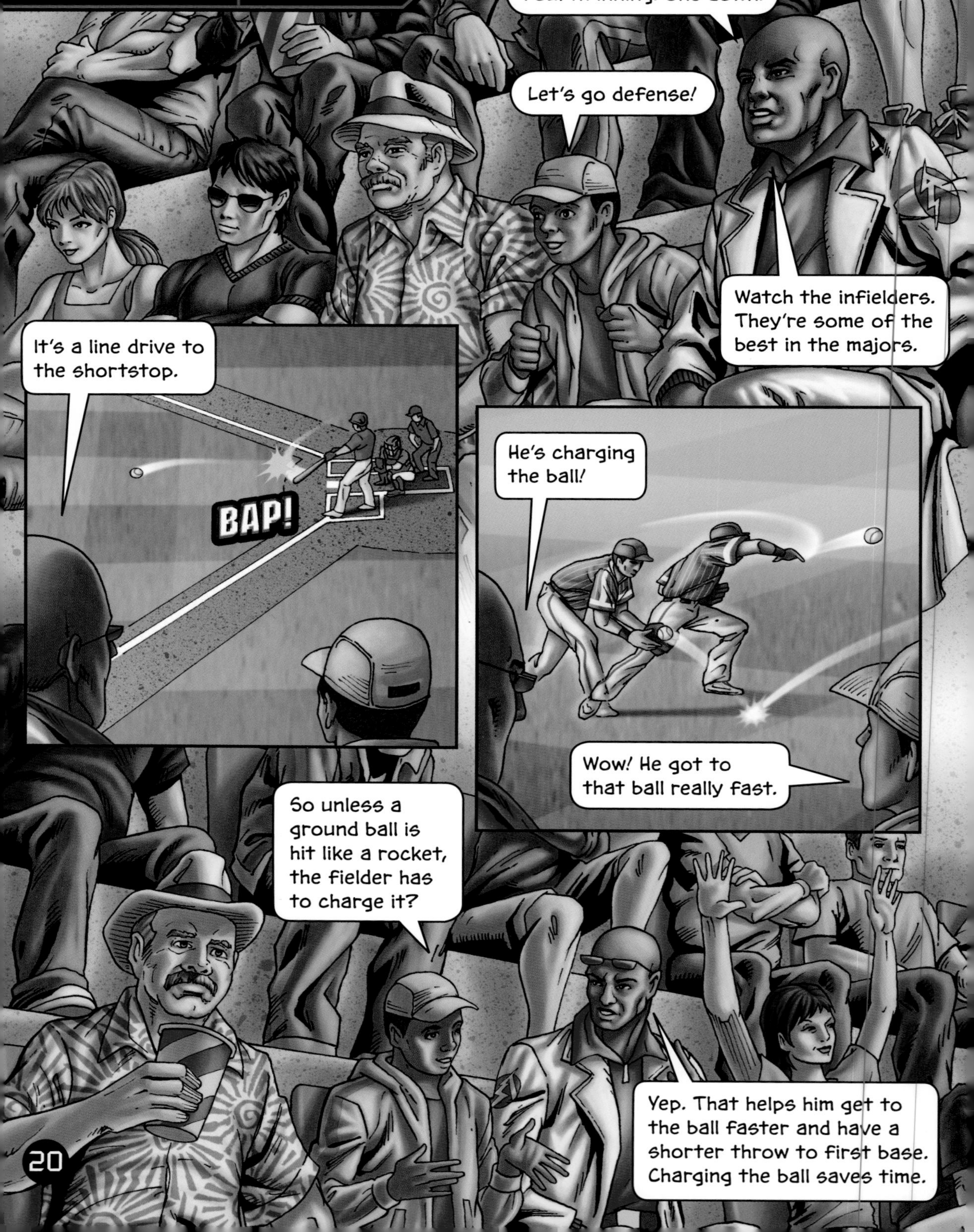
Fourth inning. One down.
Let's go defense!
Watch the infielders. They're some of the best in the majors.
It's a line drive to the shortstop.
BAP!
He's charging the ball!
Wow! He got to that ball really fast.
So unless a ground ball is hit like a rocket, the fielder has to charge it?
Yep. That helps him get to the ball faster and have a shorter throw to first base. Charging the ball saves time.

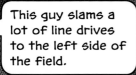
This guy slams a lot of line drives to the left side of the field.

Just like I told you!

THWACK!

Okay! Three up, three down!

WHAP!

Why did the shortstop pull his hands to his chest when he caught the ball?

That ball was moving about 110 miles an hour. The backward motion of the fielder's hands gave the ball more time to get from full speed to full stop.

I get it! That tiny bit of time decreased the force of the ball on the guy's glove. Pure physics!

Baseball gloves changed throughout the 1900s. Every improvement in them made life easier for fielders. Padding provided force-reducing cushioning from fast-moving balls. Webbing between the thumb and index finger allowed fielders to snag balls without the ball smacking into their palms.

21

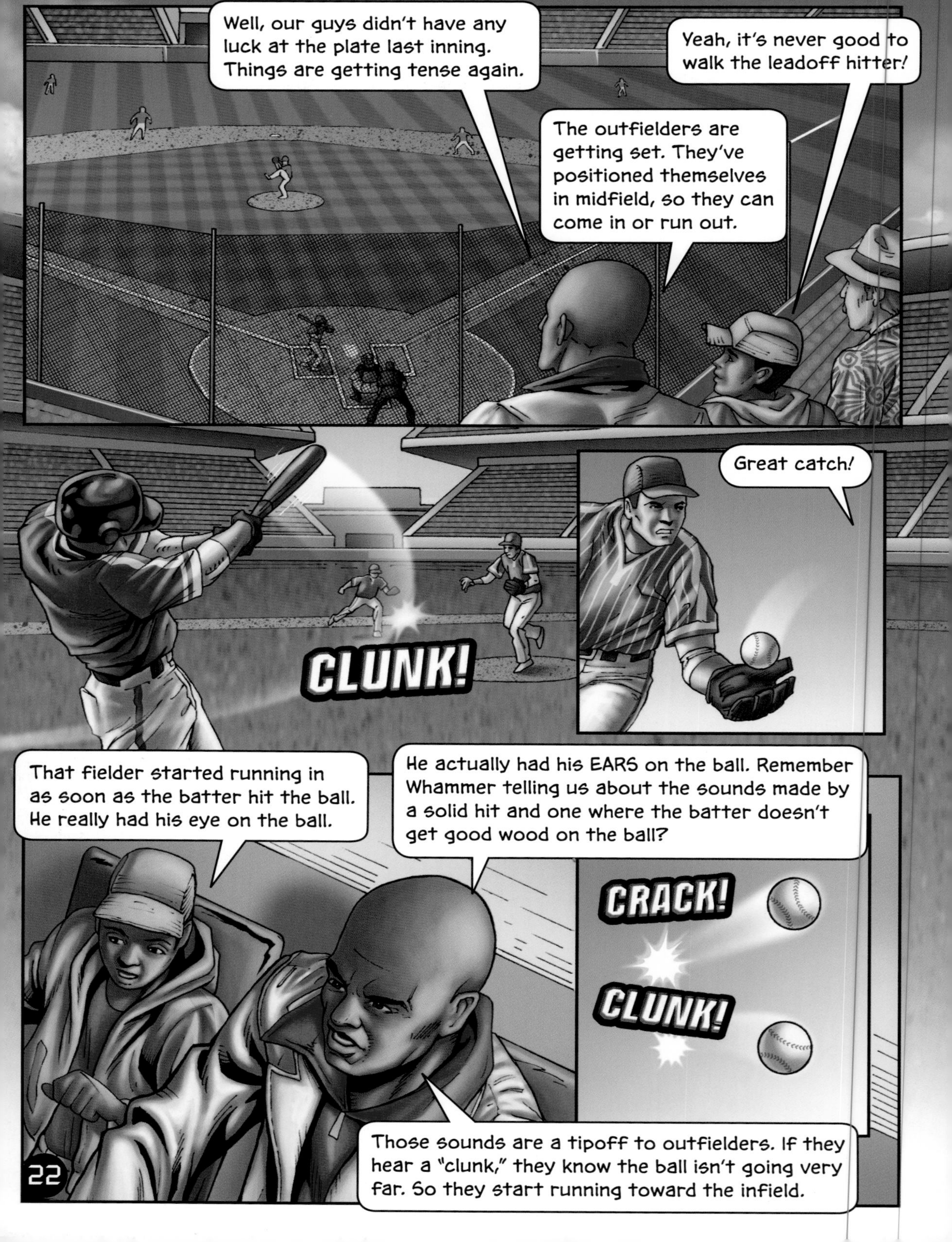
Well, our guys didn't have any luck at the plate last inning. Things are getting tense again.
Yeah, it's never good to walk the leadoff hitter!
The outfielders are getting set. They've positioned themselves in midfield, so they can come in or run out.
CLUNK!
Great catch!
That fielder started running in as soon as the batter hit the ball. He really had his eye on the ball.
He actually had his EARS on the ball. Remember Whammer telling us about the sounds made by a solid hit and one where the batter doesn't get good wood on the ball?
CRACK!
CLUNK!
Those sounds are a tipoff to outfielders. If they hear a "clunk," they know the ball isn't going very far. So they start running toward the infield.

This guy is trouble. He's been killing the ball lately.

The fielder knew as soon as he heard the hit that it was a solid one. It was going to be a long drive. If he had waited to see where the ball was heading, he wouldn't have a chance to make the catch.

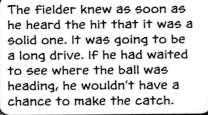

CRACK!

Wow, another fantastic catch!

That long fly advanced the runner to second base. If this next batter gets a well-placed single to center, the runner will be dashing for home.

If that happens, watch the center fielder through your stop-motion glasses. You'll see more science in action.

There you go, single to center!

It's gonna be a long throw.

The right-handed fielder snags the ball with his glove on the first bounce.

He brings his arms up to his chest and steps forward with his left foot.

He makes a slight hop to transfer his weight onto his back leg.

He leans back on his trailing leg and cocks his throwing arm, raising the front leg, bent at knee.

He brings his body weight forward, transferring his weight onto his front leg and starts to bring his arm around.

CLICK!

CLICK!

CLICK!

CLICK!

CLICK!

CLICK!

CLICK!

He fires the ball toward the infield with all the force he has generated.

Got him! Now our team is up to bat.

That's called a crow hop. It allows the fielder to generate throwing force in his body, much like a pitcher does.

He generated plenty of it. That was some throw!

Yeah, but the crow hop takes time—about a second and a half. The outfielder just barely got that runner.

Some coaches think it's better for the outfielder to just grab the ball and throw it to an infielder. Then the infielder will relay the ball to the plate.

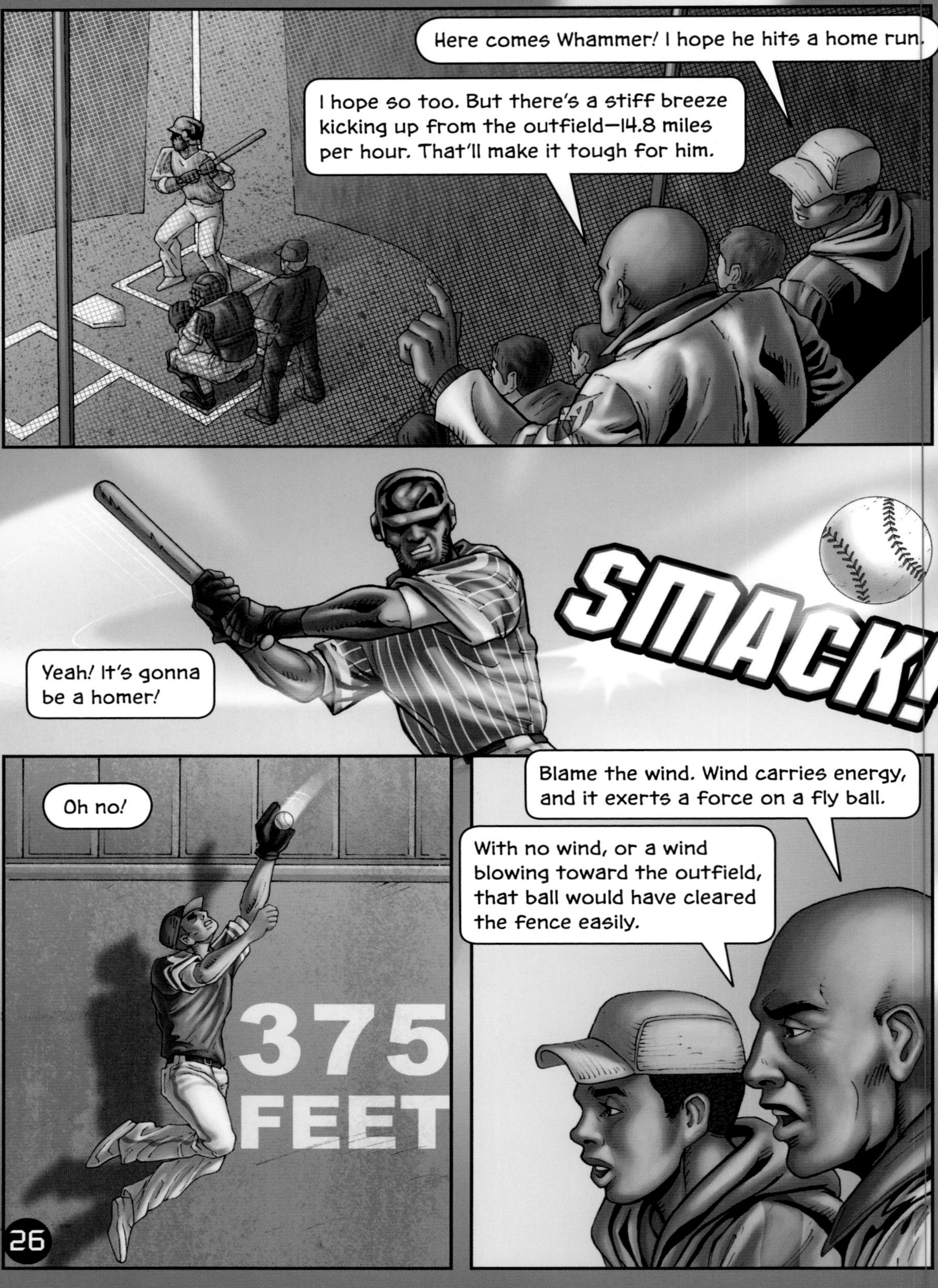
Here comes Whammer! I hope he hits a home run.
I hope so too. But there's a stiff breeze kicking up from the outfield—14.8 miles per hour. That'll make it tough for him.
SMACK!
Yeah! It's gonna be a homer!
Oh no!
375 FEET
Blame the wind. Wind carries energy, and it exerts a force on a fly ball.
With no wind, or a wind blowing toward the outfield, that ball would have cleared the fence easily.

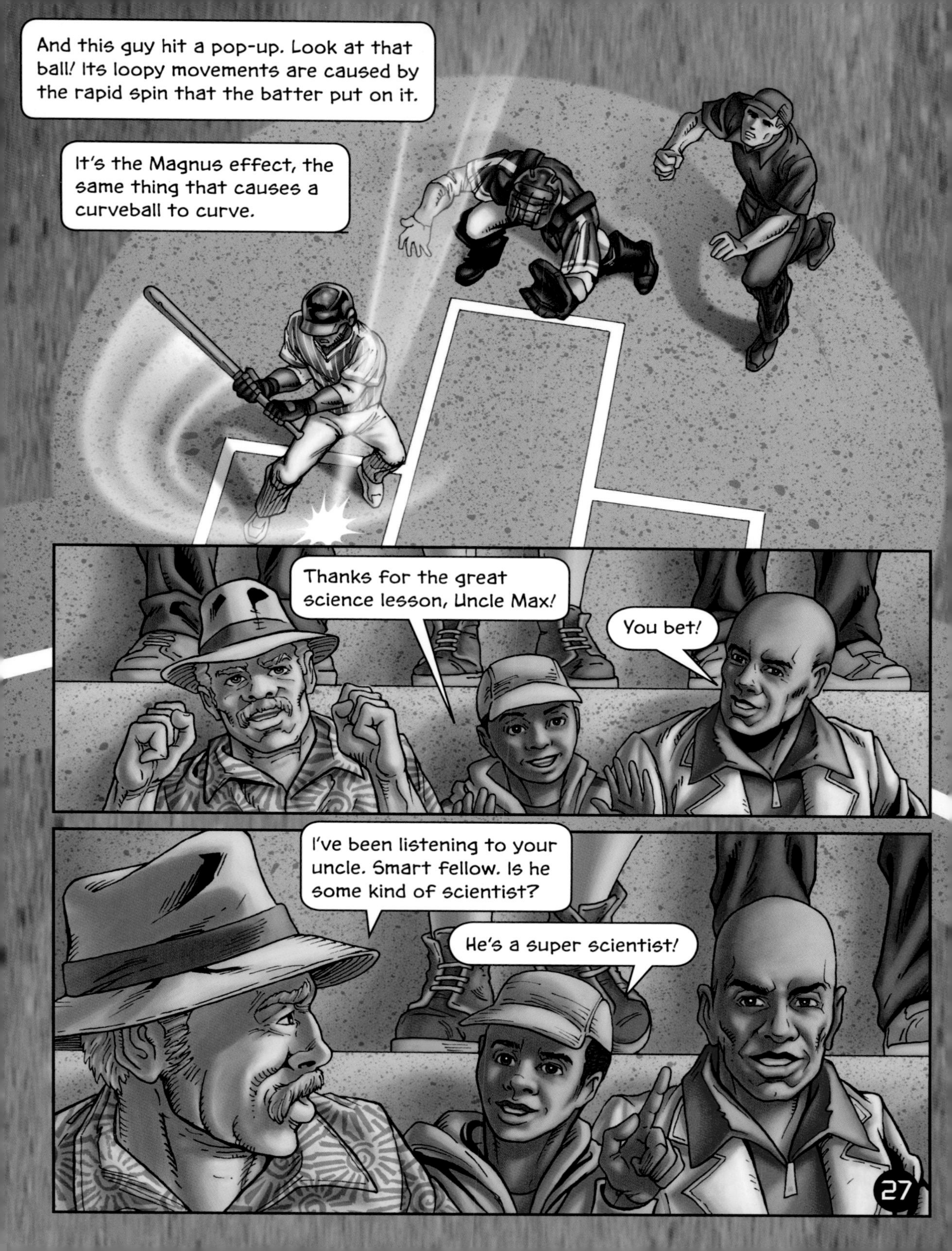
And this guy hit a pop-up. Look at that ball! Its loopy movements are caused by the rapid spin that the batter put on it.
It's the Magnus effect, the same thing that causes a curveball to curve.
Thanks for the great science lesson, Uncle Max!
You bet!
I've been listening to your uncle. Smart fellow. Is he some kind of scientist?
He's a super scientist!
27

The cork-centered baseball became standard in the major leagues in 1911. This ball was livelier than the ones that had been used previously and could thus be hit farther.

One of the hardest pitches to hit—or catch—is the knuckleball. This pitch is thrown so that it rotates very slowly. Air currents moving across the seams of the ball cause it to move inconsistently. A knuckleball is said to "flutter" or "dance" on its way to the plate.

Many pitchers suffer from repetitive-stress injuries to the soft tissues of the elbow and shoulder. One of the worst stress-related injuries to a pitcher's shoulder is called a labrum tear. The labrum is a layer of cartilage that, with ligaments, keeps the upper arm bone properly connected to the shoulder. A torn labrum requires surgery, which often is not completely successful. A labrum tear can end a pitcher's career.

Batters often insist that a fastball rises or "hops" a few inches when nearing the plate. But physicists explain that a baseball cannot rise on its way to the plate. All overhand pitches drop continually from the force of gravity. But if a pitch comes to the plate faster than a batter expects, it will drop less than he anticipates. That difference in height makes the ball appear to rise.

For most of baseball's history, the only way to measure the distance of a home run hit out of a park was with a tape measure. In recent years, however, special cameras and computer programs have made it possible to measure long hits electronically. These systems can also determine how far a home run that hits an obstacle would have traveled.

MORE ABOUT

SUPER SCIENTIST

Real name: Maxwell J. Axiom
Hometown: Seattle, Washington
Height: 6' 1"   Weight: 192 lbs
Eyes: Brown   Hair: None

Super capabilities: Super intelligence; able to shrink to the size of an atom; sunglasses give x-ray vision; lab coat allows for travel through time and space.

Origin: Since birth, Max Axiom seemed destined for greatness. His mother, a marine biologist, taught her son about the mysteries of the sea. His father, a nuclear physicist and volunteer park ranger, schooled Max on the wonders of earth and sky.

One day on a wilderness hike, a megacharged lightning bolt struck Max with blinding fury. When he awoke, Max discovered a newfound energy and set out to learn as much about science as possible. He traveled the globe earning degrees in every aspect of the field. Upon his return, he was ready to share his knowledge and new identity with the world. He had become Max Axiom, Super Scientist.

GLOSSARY

center of mass (SEN-tur UV MASS)—the point around which all of an object's mass, or weight, is evenly distributed

crow hop (KRO HOPP)—a series of motions an outfielder uses to generate force in his body and transfer it to the baseball for a long throw

energy (EH-ner-jee)—the ability to do work

force (FORS)—an act that changes the movement of an object

inertia (ih-NER-shuh)—tendency of an object to remain either at rest or in motion unless affected by an outside force

lever (LEH-ver)—a tool that multiplies or changes the direction of an applied force; a crowbar is an example of a lever

Magnus effect (MAG-nuhs uh-FEKT)—a force produced by differences in air pressure around a spinning object

moment of inertia (MOH-ment UV ih-NER-shuh)—a measure of how hard it is to change the speed of an object rotating around a pivot point; a bat with a high moment of inertia is harder to swing than a bat with a low moment of inertia

momentum (moh-MEN-tum)—the amount of force in a moving object determined by the object's mass and speed

pivot point (PIH-vut POYNT)—a point about six inches above the knob of a bat around which the bat is swung

sweet spot (SWEET SPOT)—the place on a bat where a hit is most solid and produces the least amount of vibration

swing weight (SWING WATE)—the "feel" of a bat in a batter's hands; bats of the same actual weight can have different swing weights depending on how their mass is distributed

READ MORE

Adamson, Thomas K. *Baseball: the Math of the Game.* Sports Illustrated KIDS. Mankato, Minn.: Capstone Sports, 2012.

Dreier, David L. *Baseball: How It Works.* The Science of Sports. Mankato, Minn.: Capstone Press, 2010.

Graubart, Norman D. *The Science of Baseball.* Sports Science. New York: PowerKids Press, 2016.

Hetrick, Hans. *Play Baseball Like a Pro: Key Skills and Tips.* Play Like the Pros. Mankato, Minn.: Capstone Press, 2011.

INTERNET SITES

FactHound offers a safe, fun way to find Internet sites related to this book. All sites on FactHound have been researched by our staff.

Here's all you do:

Visit *www.facthound.com*

Type in this code: 9781491460832

 Check out projects, games and lots more at **www.capstonekids.com**

INDEX

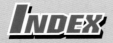